Comprehension Skills

Level 1
English

Text copyright © 2005 Linda Ward Beech

Illustration copyright © 2005 Scholastic Inc.

Copyright © 2013 Scholastic Education International (Singapore) Private Limited
All rights reserved.

Previously published as Reading Passages that Build Comprehension

This edition published by Scholastic Education International (Singapore) Private Limited
A division of Scholastic Inc.

First edition 2013

ISBN 978-981-07-3285-1

Welcome to ■SCHOLASTIC studySMⒶRT !

Comprehension Skills provides opportunities for structured and repeated practice of specific reading skills at age-appropriate levels to help your child develop comprehension skills.

It is often a challenge to help a child develop the different types of reading skills, especially as he encounters an increasing variety of texts. The age-appropriate and engaging texts will encourage your child to read and sift out the important information essential to read specific kinds of texts. As your child progresses through the levels, he will encounter a greater variety of skills and texts while continuing to practice previously learnt skills at a more difficult level to ensure mastery.

Every section targets a specific reading skill and the repeated practice of the skill ensures your child masters the reading skill. There are extension activities that can be done for specific reading skills to encourage your child to delve even deeper into the texts.

How to use this book?

1. Introduce the target reading skill at the beginning of each section to your child.

2. Let your child complete the reading exercises.

3. Reinforce your child's learning with an extension activity at the end of each activity. These activities provide additional practice, and extend your child's learning of the particular reading skill.

Note: To avoid the awkward 'he or she' construction, the pronouns in this book will refer to the male gender.

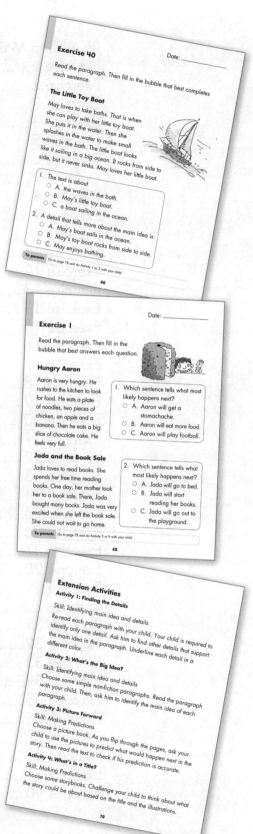

3

Contents

Identifying Main Ideas and Supporting Details

Reading comprehension involves numerous thinking skills. Identifying main ideas and the details that support them is one such skill. A reader who is adept at identifying main ideas makes better sense of a text and increases his comprehension of what is being communicated. The passages and questions in this section will help your child learn to recognize main ideas and the details that develop them.

Understanding the main idea of a passage is to be able to have a broad overall understanding of what a passage is all about. This section will provide opportunities for your child to understand that supporting details fill in information about the main idea and that the main idea is bigger and broader than the supporting details.

The extension activities provide additional challenges to your child to encourage and develop his understanding of the particular comprehension skill.

Exercise 1

Read the paragraph. Then fill in the bubble that best completes each sentence.

Birthday Cake

My sister Lisa is three years old today. My parents got her a birthday cake. It is a strawberry cake. The cake is pink in color. It has little roses on it. There are three big blue candles on the cake.

1. The text is about
   ○ A. birthday cakes.
   ○ B. Lisa's birthday cake.
   ○ C. Lisa, the writer's sister.

2. A detail that tells about the main idea is:
   ○ A. The cake is blue.
   ○ B. The cake has small roses on it.
   ○ C. There are four candles on the cake.

To parents Go to page 78 and do Activity 1 or 2 with your child.

Exercise 2

Read the paragraph. Then fill in the bubble that best completes each sentence.

My Best Friend Rachel

My best friend's name is Rachel Westwood. She is tall and thin. She has long brown hair. She likes to tie her hair in two pigtails. She is a very kind person. In school, she always shares her food and toys with me. Rachel and I do everything together. Every day we eat, play and study together. I hope we will always be friends.

1. The text is about
   - ○ A. sharing toys.
   - ○ B. good friends.
   - ○ C. Rachel, the writer's best friend.

2. A detail that tells about the main idea is:
   - ○ A. They always fight.
   - ○ B. Rachel ties her hair in a ponytail.
   - ○ C. They eat, play and study together every day.

To parents   Go to page 78 and do Activity 1 or 2 with your child.

Exercise 3

Read the paragraph. Then fill in the bubble that best completes each sentence.

Daddy

My daddy loves me very much. He plays games with me when he comes home from work. Sometimes we play football in the field. On other days, we go cycling. When Daddy is tired, we just go for a walk in the park. I love my daddy. He is the best daddy in the world.

1. The text is about
   ○ A. good fathers.
   ○ B. the writer's love for his daddy.
   ○ C. walking, cycling and playing football.

2. A detail that tells about the main idea is:
   ○ A. His daddy is very busy at work.
   ○ B. They don't spend time together.
   ○ C. He goes for walks, cycles and plays football with his daddy.

To parents Go to page 78 and do Activity 1 or 2 with your child.

Exercise 4

Read the paragraph. Then fill in the bubble that best completes each sentence.

A Christmas Party

Robert and James are going to a Christmas party. They are wearing red and green shirts. They are taking some presents to the party. They will give them to their friends. They are also taking some fruit cakes and minced pies for the party. They are very excited. They have big smiles on their faces.

1. The text is about
   - ○ A. green and red Christmas clothes.
   - ○ B. Christmas parties around the world.
   - ○ C. the Christmas party Robert and James are going to.

2. A detail that tells about the main idea is:
   - ○ A. Robert and James are unhappy.
   - ○ B. Robert and James are taking fruits to the party.
   - ○ C. Robert and James are wearing green and red clothes.

To parents Go to page 78 and do Activity 1 or 2 with your child.

Exercise 5

Read the paragraph. Then fill in the bubble that best completes each sentence.

The Farm

Laura visited an animal farm yesterday. On the farm she saw many animals. There were chickens, goats, cows, ducks, and horses on the farm. The farmer let Laura play with all the animals. Then Laura helped him feed the animals. She was very happy she could help with the animals. Laura hopes she can visit again someday.

1. The text is about
   - ○ A. farm animals.
   - ○ B. feeding animals.
   - ○ C. Laura's farm visit.

2. A detail that tells about the main idea is:
   - ○ A. Laura rode animals on the farm.
   - ○ B. Laura helped to feed the animals.
   - ○ C. Laura does not want to go back to the farm.

To parents Go to page 78 and do Activity 1 or 2 with your child.

Exercise 6

Read the paragraph. Then fill in the bubble that best completes each sentence.

Shopping with Mummy

Jane loves shopping with her mummy. Today she went to buy flowers with her mummy. At the florist, Jane saw many different flowers. The flowers were of different colors. Jane helped her mummy choose some red and orange flowers for their vase. Her mother also bought some white and pink flowers for Jane's grandmother.

1. The text is about
   - ○ A. white and pink flowers.
   - ○ B. shopping with mummy.
   - ○ C. shopping for flowers with mummy.

2. A detail that tells more about the main idea is:
   - ○ A. Jane did not want to go shopping.
   - ○ B. Jane saw only white and pink flowers.
   - ○ C. Jane chose red and orange flowers for her mummy.

To parents Go to page 78 and do Activity 1 or 2 with your child.

Exercise 7

Read the paragraph. Then fill in the bubble that best completes each sentence.

Fun at the Fun Fair

The fun fair is near Kevin's home. Every day Kevin visits the fun fair with his brother, John. He loves to sit on the Ferris wheel with John. You can hear them laughing as they go up the Ferris wheel. At the fun fair, John buys Kevin his favorite cotton floss candy. He becomes very happy after visiting the fun fair.

1. The text is about
   ○ A. fun fairs.
   ○ B. riding the Ferris wheel.
   ○ C. Kevin enjoying the fun fair.

2. A detail that tells more about the main idea is:
   ○ A. Kevin is tired after visiting the fun fair.
   ○ B. Kevin and John laugh on the Ferris wheel.
   ○ C. Kevin takes good care of John at the fun fair.

To parents Go to page 78 and do Activity 1 or 2 with your child.

Exercise 8

Read the paragraph. Then fill in the bubble that best completes each sentence.

The Picnic

It is a sunny morning. Gina is going for a picnic. She is taking a picnic basket with her. She has a brown picnic basket. It is a beautiful basket. In the  basket Gina has some cold lemonade, cucumber sandwiches, and a slice of cheese cake. Gina is excited about her picnic.

1. The text is about
    ○ A. Gina going on a picnic.
    ○ B. Gina and her food.
    ○ C. fun at picnics.

2. A detail that tells more about the main idea is:
    ○ A. Gina's food is in a box.
    ○ B. Gina has drinks and food in her picnic basket.
    ○ C. Gina thinks she will not enjoy her picnic.

To parents Go to page 78 and do Activity 1 or 2 with your child.

Exercise 9

Read the paragraph. Then fill in the bubble that best completes each sentence.

It's Bath Time

Andy always enjoys his bath time. He does not cry when he has his bath. He loves to play with the bubbles in his bath. There are also three rubber ducks in Andy's bath. He usually fills them up with water and lets them float around him. This makes Andy squeal with laughter.

1. The text is about
   - ○ A. rubber ducks in the bath tub.
   - ○ B. Andy having fun during bath time.
   - ○ C. bathing.

2. A detail that tells more about the main idea is:
   - ○ A. Andy cries while bathing.
   - ○ B. there are plastic crabs in his bath tub.
   - ○ C. Andy squeals with laughter while bathing.

To parents   Go to page 78 and do Activity 1 or 2 with your child.

Exercise 10

Read the paragraph. Then fill in the bubble that best completes each sentence.

Circus Mania

Mr Ballino's circus is in town. There are monkeys, lions and elephants at the circus. The animals in Mr Ballino's circus are special. They are able to do many tricks. The elephants can play with balls. The monkeys can ride bicycles. All the children can't wait to visit his circus.

1. The text is about
   - ○ A. animals in a circus.
   - ○ B. Mr Ballino's special circus.
   - ○ C. the circus being in town.

2. A detail that tells more about the main idea is:
   - ○ A. There are monkeys, snakes, and giraffes at the circus.
   - ○ B. The elephants can play with sticks.
   - ○ C. The monkeys can ride bicycles.

To parents Go to page 78 and do Activity 1 or 2 with your child.

Exercise 11

Read the paragraph. Then fill in the bubble that best completes each sentence.

Camping

The scouts are going camping this
weekend. They have to make sure they
bring all the necessary equipment. They
have to pack enough food and water. They

also have to bring their own camping tents. All the scouts are excited
about their camping trip. They are looking forward to the weekend.

1. The text is about
    ○ A. scouts camping in the jungle.
    ○ B. scouts getting ready for a camping trip.
    ○ C. scouts having fun.

2. A detail that tells more about the main idea is:
    ○ A. The scouts are worried about the trip.
    ○ B. The scouts need to buy sleeping bags.
    ○ C. The scouts need to bring their own
         camping tents.

To parents   Go to page 78 and do Activity 1 or 2 with your child.

Exercise 12

Read the paragraph. Then fill in the bubble that best completes each sentence.

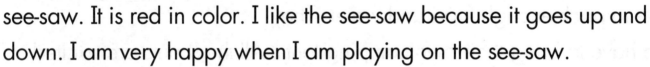

The Playground

There is a wonderful playground next
to my house. It has a slide, a see-saw,
and a swing. I enjoy playing on the
see-saw. It is red in color. I like the see-saw because it goes up and
down. I am very happy when I am playing on the see-saw.

1. The text is about
   - ○ A. the writer enjoying the playground.
   - ○ B. the writer's see-saw in his garden.
   - ○ C. the writer's first visit to the playground.

2. A detail that tells more about the main idea is:
   - ○ A. The writer enjoys playing on the see-saw.
   - ○ B. The playground has a slide, see-saw and
     merry-go-round.
   - ○ C. The playground is far away from the
     writer's house.

To parents   Go to page 78 and do Activity 1 or 2 with your child.

Exercise 13

Read the paragraph. Then fill in the bubble that best completes each sentence.

Peaches the Cat

My cat's name is Peaches. It is a black and white cat with brown eyes. Peaches is a very loving cat. She sleeps on my bed every night. She is also very clever. She can do tricks with her ball and climb very high walls. I am very proud of Peaches.

1. The text is about
   - ○ A. peaches.
   - ○ B. Peaches the cat.
   - ○ C. neighborhood cats.

2. A detail that tells more about the main idea is:
   - ○ A. Peaches has brown eyes.
   - ○ B. Peaches is a brown cat.
   - ○ C. Peaches is lazy.

To parents   Go to page 78 and do Activity 1 or 2 with your child.

Exercise 14

Read the paragraph. Then fill in the bubble that best completes each sentence.

My Teacher

Miss Melissa is my favorite teacher. I like her because she is kind and helpful. She helps me with my drawing and coloring. She cheers me up and makes me happy if I miss mummy and daddy in school. Miss Melissa is also very pretty. She is a tall lady. She has long, dark brown hair. She is the best teacher in the world!

1. The text is about
   ○ A. teachers in school.
   ○ B. drawing and coloring in school.
   ○ C. Miss Melissa, the writer's beloved teacher.

2. A detail that tells more about the main idea is:
   ○ A. Miss Melissa is short.
   ○ B. Miss Melissa makes the writer happy.
   ○ C. Miss Melissa helps the writer to read and write.

To parents Go to page 78 and do Activity 1 or 2 with your child.

Exercise 15

Read the paragraph. Then fill in the bubble that best completes each sentence.

Sports Day

Allan is a very active and energetic boy. Today was sports day in his school. He enjoyed sports day very much. Allan won three medals at his sports day. He won a gold medal for the high jump. He won a  silver medal for the 50-meter sprint. He also won a bronze medal for a group race. Allan's parents were very proud of him.

1. The text is about
   - ○ A. sports at school.
   - ○ B. Allan's experience at sports day.
   - ○ C. Allan's parents.

2. A detail that tells more about the main idea is:
   - ○ A. Allan won two medals on sports day.
   - ○ B. Allan participated in a group race.
   - ○ C. Allan's parents were unhappy with him.

To parents Go to page 78 and do Activity 1 or 2 with your child.

Exercise 16

Read the paragraph. Then fill in the bubble that best completes each sentence.

Coffee Coffee!

Justin's mother enjoys drinking coffee. She drinks coffee every day. When she wakes up in the morning, she drinks one cup of coffee. In the afternoon, she drinks two cups of coffee. In the evening, she drinks another cup. She has to buy coffee once a week from the supermarket.

1. The text is about
    ○ A. drinking coffee every day.
    ○ B. Justin's mother enjoying drinking coffee.
    ○ C. buying coffee every week.

2. A detail that tells more about the main idea is:
    ○ A. Justin's mother drinks coffee once a week.
    ○ B. Justin has a cup of coffee in the morning.
    ○ C. Justin's mother has one cup of coffee in the morning.

To parents Go to page 78 and do Activity 1 or 2 with your child.

Exercise 17

Read the paragraph. Then fill in the bubble that best completes each sentence.

Big Breakfast

Martin enjoys having a big breakfast. He has two slices of toast with butter and jam. He also has a plate of scrambled eggs. Some mornings, he has bacon too. He finishes his breakfast with a big glass of cold milk. He is very full once he finishes eating.

1. The text is about
   - ○ A. eating a good breakfast.
   - ○ B. Martin having a large breakfast.
   - ○ C. having eggs for breakfast.

2. A detail that tells more about the main idea is:
   - ○ A. Martin does not eat breakfast.
   - ○ B. Martin eats two slices of bread with butter and jam.
   - ○ C. Martin is still hungry after eating breakfast.

To parents   Go to page 78 and do Activity 1 or 2 with your child.

Exercise 18

Read the paragraph. Then fill in the bubble that best completes each sentence.

A Beautiful Rainbow

David saw a rainbow today. The rainbow appeared after the rain. David tried to count the different colors in that rainbow. Some of these colors were blue, red, yellow, green, and orange. Red is the brightest color in the rainbow. Red is also David's favorite color in the rainbow.

1. The text is about
   - ○ A. the colors of a rainbow.
   - ○ B. David's favorite color.
   - ○ C. the beautiful rainbow David saw.

2. A detail that tells more about the main idea is:
   - ○ A. David saw blue, red, yellow, green and orange in the rainbow.
   - ○ B. David's favorite color in the rainbow is blue.
   - ○ C. David does not like rainbows.

To parents Go to page 78 and do Activity 1 or 2 with your child.

Exercise 19

Read the paragraph. Then fill in the bubble that best completes each sentence.

A Trip to the Zoo

Ethan visited the zoo with his brother Ryan. He saw many animals there. Most of the animals were in large enclosures. Ethan was allowed to feed the animals. He chose to feed the monkeys. He gave the monkeys some bananas. It was a lot of fun.

1. The text is about
    - ○ A. feeding monkeys.
    - ○ B. animals at the zoo.
    - ○ C. Ethan and Ryan's visit to the zoo.

2. A detail that tells more about the main idea is:
    - ○ A. Ryan fed a giraffe.
    - ○ B. Ethan fed the monkeys bananas.
    - ○ C. Ethan only saw a few animals.

To parents Go to page 78 and do Activity 1 or 2 with your child.

Exercise 20

Read the paragraph. Then fill in the bubble that best completes each sentence.

Getting Ready for School

Today is Zoe's first day of school. She is very nervous. Her mother bought her a new school bag. It is a pink bag. She has new books in her bag. Zoe also has a new school uniform. Her shoes and socks are sparkling white. Zoe is ready for her first day of school.

1. The text is about
   ○ A. a new school bag.
   ○ B. Zoe's first day at school.
   ○ C. getting ready for school every morning.

2. A detail that tells more about the main idea is:
   ○ A. Zoe has a new pink school bag.
   ○ B. Zoe's shoes are black.
   ○ C. Zoe likes to go to school.

To parents Go to page 78 and do Activity 1 or 2 with your child.

Exercise 21

Read the paragraph. Then fill in the bubble that best completes each sentence.

Learning How to Bowl

Today is Anne's first day of learning how to bowl. First, she takes the bowling ball in two hands. Next she places her fingers into the ball. Then she swings and throws the ball. Anne knocks down four pins on her first try. Good job, Anne!

1. The text is about
   - ○ A. learning to play a new game.
   - ○ B. Anne' first try at bowling.
   - ○ C. bowling as a sport.

2. A detail that tells more about the main idea is:
   - ○ A. Anne knocks down four pins on her first throw.
   - ○ B. Bowling is hard.
   - ○ C. Anne uses her feet to bowl.

To parents Go to page 78 and do Activity 1 or 2 with your child.

Exercise 22

Read the paragraph. Then fill in the bubble that best completes each sentence.

Painting Like Picasso

Lucas wants to be a famous painter like Pablo Picasso. He loves painting color on paper. Everywhere he goes, he collects different paint colors. He now has blue, yellow, green, black, and orange paints. The last picture he painted was a ship. His teacher said it was brilliant!

1. The text is about
   - ○ A. painting ships.
   - ○ B. Lucas's love for painting.
   - ○ C. Pablo Picasso.

2. A detail that tells more about the main idea is:
   - ○ A. Lucas likes painting on canvas.
   - ○ B. Lucas only loves to paint ships.
   - ○ C. Lucas paints in many different paint colors.

To parents   Go to page 78 and do Activity 1 or 2 with your child.

Exercise 23

Read the paragraph. Then fill in the bubble that best completes each sentence.

Black Beauty

Jane loves horses. She named her horse Black Beauty. It is a black and beautiful horse. It is also a good and friendly horse. It can go very fast. When Jane rides Black Beauty, she feels happy. Jane rides her horse once every week.

1. The text is about
   - ○ A. black horses.
   - ○ B. fast horses.
   - ○ C. Jane's horse Black Beauty.

2. A detail that tells more about the main idea is:
   - ○ A. Black Beauty is a friendly horse.
   - ○ B. Black Beauty is a slow-moving horse.
   - ○ C. Jane is afraid to ride her horse.

To parents   Go to page 78 and do Activity 1 or 2 with your child.

Exercise 24

Read the paragraph. Then fill in the bubble that best completes each sentence.

Sing Along

Elisa has a beautiful voice. She can sing very well. Elisa sings everywhere she goes. She sings in her school choir. Her choir teacher thinks Elisa has a beautiful voice. She says Elisa sounds like a lark. She makes Elisa the lead singer.

1. The paragraph is about
    ○ A. Elisa's choir teacher.
    ○ B. joining the choir.
    ○ C. Elisa's beautiful voice.

2. A detail that tells more about the main idea is:
    ○ A. Elisa sings at home.
    ○ B. Her teacher says Elisa sings like a lark.
    ○ C. Elisa is not in the choir.

To parents   Go to page 78 and do Activity 1 or 2 with your child.

Exercise 25

Read the paragraph. Then fill in the bubble that best completes each sentence.

Handbags!!!

My mother has many handbags. Her whole cupboard is full of handbags. Her handbags come in different sizes. There are long handbags. There are small handbags. There are also round handbags. Her handbags also come in different colors. Black is my mother's favorite color. She has many black handbags.

1. The text is about
    - ○ A. black handbags.
    - ○ B. the writer's mother's handbags.
    - ○ C. the writer's handbags.

2. A detail that tells more about the main idea is:
    - ○ A. The writer's mother has square handbags.
    - ○ B. The writer's mother has few handbags.
    - ○ C. The cupboard is full of the writer's mother's handbags.

To parents Go to page 78 and do Activity 1 or 2 with your child.

Exercise 26

Read the paragraph. Then fill in the bubble that best completes each sentence.

My Favorite Singer

My name is Jacob. I am 11 years old.
Elvis Presley is my favorite singer. I love
all of his music. He has a great voice.
I love to dance to Elvis Presley's music.
Every morning, I listen to his music.
I listen to his music while eating breakfast. Elvis Presley is the best!

1. The text is about
   - ○ A. eating breakfast with Elvis Presley.
   - ○ B. dancing to Elvis Presley's music.
   - ○ C. Jacob's favorite singer, Elvis Presley.

2. A detail that tells more about the main idea is:
   - ○ A. Elvis Presley is 11 years old.
   - ○ B. Jacob dances to Elvis' music.
   - ○ C. Jacob eats breakfast alone.

To parents   Go to page 78 and do Activity 1 or 2 with your child.

Date: _____

Exercise 27

Read the paragraph. Then fill in the bubble that best completes each sentence.

My Trip to the Market

Today is Saturday. In the morning, I go to the fish market with my mother. She buys many things at the market. First, my mother buys two big fishes. Next, she

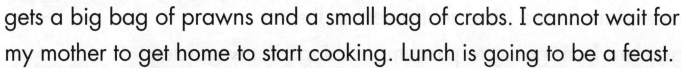

gets a big bag of prawns and a small bag of crabs. I cannot wait for my mother to get home to start cooking. Lunch is going to be a feast.

1. The text is about
   ○ A. cooking crabs.
   ○ B. lunch being a feast.
   ○ C. going to the market with Mother.

2. A detail that tells more about the main idea is:
   ○ A. Mother buys two big fishes.
   ○ B. Mother cooks crabs for dinner.
   ○ C. Mother buys two big bags of prawns.

To parents Go to page 78 and do Activity 1 or 2 with your child.

Exercise 28

Read the paragraph. Then fill in the bubble that best completes each sentence.

My Garden

My name is Jenny. I have a beautiful garden in my house. I water the plants in my garden every evening. I have a rose plant in my garden. It is a yellow rose plant. I also have sunflowers in the garden. I am going to plant more things in my garden.

1. The text is about
   ○ A. Jenny's beautiful garden.
   ○ B. a rose garden.
   ○ C. sunflowers in the garden.

2. A detail that tells more about the main idea is:
   ○ A. Jenny has yellow roses in her garden.
   ○ B. Jenny has red roses in her garden.
   ○ C. Jenny waters her garden once a week.

To parents   Go to page 78 and do Activity 1 or 2 with your child.

Date: _____

Exercise 29

Read the paragraph. Then fill in the bubble that best completes each sentence.

My Family

A family can be of any size. My family is a big family. I have a brother named Daniel. My sisters' names are Ginny, Jenny and Penny. We live in a big house with my parents and grandparents. We also have pets in our family. We have a big dog named Pongo. Our little kitten's name is Topsy.

1. The text is about
   - ○ A. the writer's big family.
   - ○ B. a small family.
   - ○ C. pets in the writer's family.

2. A detail that tells more about the main idea is:
   - ○ A. the writer has three sisters.
   - ○ B. the writer has two brothers.
   - ○ C. the writer does not live with her grandparents.

To parents   Go to page 78 and do Activity 1 or 2 with your child.

Exercise 30

Read the paragraph. Then fill in the bubble that best completes each sentence.

A Holiday

I am going for a holiday with my family. We are going to Mauritius. My mother has packed all our bags. We have beachwear and slippers for the holiday. We are very excited to go on this holiday. We are bringing a camera. We will take many photographs during the holiday.

1. The text is about
   - ○ A. new clothes and shoes.
   - ○ B. going on a holiday with the family.
   - ○ C. going for an outing to the beach.

2. A detail that tells more about the main idea is:
   - ○ A. They have a camera.
   - ○ B. They have warm clothing.
   - ○ C. They are unhappy about the holiday.

To parents   Go to page 78 and do Activity 1 or 2 with your child.

Exercise 31

Read the paragraph. Then fill in the bubble that best completes each sentence.

The Bus

Today was Jimmy's first day of taking the school bus. He was very nervous. He was afraid he would lose his way. He waited at the bus stop. When he saw the bus, he put his hand out to stop it. When the bus stopped, Jimmy slowly climbed onto the bus. He smiled at the bus driver. When he took his seat, he sighed with relief.

1. The text is about
   - ○ A. Jimmy's first day at school.
   - ○ B. Jimmy's first time taking the school bus.
   - ○ C. taking the school bus.

2. A detail that tells more about the main idea is:
   - ○ A. Jimmy was excited.
   - ○ B. Jimmy was afraid of losing his way.
   - ○ C. Jimmy asked the bus driver for help.

To parents Go to page 78 and do Activity 1 or 2 with your child.

Exercise 32

Read the paragraph. Then fill in the bubble
that best completes each sentence.

New Shoes

Amanda needs a new pair of shoes for school.
Her old pair is torn. Her old shoes have many
holes in them. They are also very dirty. Today,
Amanda goes to the shoe shop with her mother.
Her mother buys her a new pair of shoes. They
are sparkling white. Amanda is looking forward to school on Monday!

1. The text is about
   - ○ A. Amanda needing a new pair of shoes.
   - ○ B. Amanda going to school on Monday.
   - ○ C. Amanda going to the shops with her mother.

2. A detail that tells more about the main idea is:
   - ○ A. Amanda's old shoes are torn.
   - ○ B. Amanda's old shoes are clean.
   - ○ C. Amanda does not like school.

To parents Go to page 78 and do Activity 1 or 2 with your child.

Exercise 33

Read the paragraph. Then fill in the bubble that best completes each sentence.

On An Airplane

This is my first time in an airplane. It is very big. It has many seats. There are small television screens behind each seat. I can watch cartoons on the screen. They serve me food and drinks. I have an orange juice with my sandwich. I like traveling on an airplane.

1. The text is about
    - ○ A. eating on an airplane.
    - ○ B. my first trip on an airplane.
    - ○ C. watching cartoons on an airplane.

2. A detail that tells more about the main idea is:
    - ○ A. An airplane has few seats.
    - ○ B. There is no food on an airplane.
    - ○ C. I can watch cartoons on an airplane.

To parents   Go to page 78 and do Activity 1 or 2 with your child.

39

Exercise 34

Read the paragraph. Then fill in the bubble that best completes each sentence.

Oh Baby My Baby

Baby Jacob is my younger brother. He is 6 months old. He is usually a happy baby. But when he is hungry, he starts to cry. It makes me sad to see him cry. When my mother gives him his milk, he stops crying. I love my brother very much.

1. The text is about
   - ○ A. crying babies.
   - ○ B. Baby Jacob.
   - ○ C. milk bottles.

2. A detail that tells more about the main idea is:
   - ○ A. Baby Jacob is always crying.
   - ○ B. Baby Jacob is a happy baby.
   - ○ C. Baby Jacob is 8 months old.

To parents Go to page 78 and do Activity 1 or 2 with your child.

Exercise 35

Read the paragraph. Then fill in the bubble that best completes each sentence.

Toys and More Toys

I visited the toy shop today. There were many toys on sale. There were trains, buses, airplanes and cars. My father said I could choose only one toy. I really wanted a toy car. I chose a yellow toy car. It reminded me of a bumble bee. I named my car Bumble Bee.

1. The text is about
   - ○ A. a toy car.
   - ○ B. a bumble bee.
   - ○ C. a toy shop.

2. A detail that tells more about the main idea is:
   - ○ A. The toy shop only had cars.
   - ○ B. The toy shop had a yellow toy car.
   - ○ C. The toy shop had toy bumble bees.

To parents Go to page 78 and do Activity 1 or 2 with your child.

Date: _____

Exercise 36

Read the paragraph. Then fill in the bubble that best completes each sentence.

Becoming a Nurse

Jean has always wanted to be a nurse. She has to do a three-year course to train as a nurse. She will have to learn how to take care of sick people. She will also have to learn to give them medicine. Jean is looking forward to becoming a nurse!

1. The text is about
   - ○ A. becoming a nurse.
   - ○ B. Jean's nurse.
   - ○ C. giving medicine.

2. A detail that tells about the main idea is:
   - ○ A. Jean has to take a three-year course.
   - ○ B. Jean needs to learn how to make medicine.
   - ○ C. Jean does not like nursing.

To parents   Go to page 78 and do Activity 1 or 2 with your child.

Exercise 37

Read the paragraph. Then fill in the bubble that best completes each sentence.

Learning How to Save

Learning how to save money at an early age is important. You should always keep aside a small part of your allowance. The best way to do this is to have a coin bank. Once the coin bank is full, you can ask your parents to take it to the bank. They can open a savings account for you.

1. The text is about
   - ○ A. saving money early.
   - ○ B. buying a coin bank.
   - ○ C. spending your allowance.

2. A detail that tells about the main idea is:
   - ○ A. You can save money using a coin bank.
   - ○ B. You can open a current account at the bank.
   - ○ C. You should spend all your allowance.

To parents Go to page 78 and do Activity 1 or 2 with your child.

Exercise 38

Read the paragraph. Then fill in the bubble that best completes each sentence.

Wind, Wind, Blow Away

It was a cold and windy day. Jeff was going to meet his friend. He put on his hat. Then he tied a scarf round his neck. He was all set. Then, a strong gust of wind blew his hat off. Up and up it went. It finally landed on top of a tree!

1. The text is about
   - ○ A. Jeff's scarf.
   - ○ B. Jeff's hat getting blown away.
   - ○ C. Jeff's meeting with his friend.

2. A detail that tells more about the main idea is:
   - ○ A. He tied a scarf round his neck.
   - ○ B. The hat landed on top of a tree.
   - ○ C. Jeff was all set to meet his friend.

To parents   Go to page 78 and do Activity 1 or 2 with your child.

Exercise 39

Read the paragraph. Then fill in the bubble that best completes each sentence.

Jim's Kite

Jim loves to fly kites. When he has time, he goes to the open field near his house. He flies his diamond-shaped kite. It is very big and it has ribbons on the end. Jim thinks it looks like a big bird in the sky.

1. The text is about
   - ○ A. The open field near Jim's house.
   - ○ B. The ribbons on Jim's kite.
   - ○ C. Jim's kite.

2. A detail that tells more about the main idea is:
   - ○ A. Jim likes to go to the field.
   - ○ B. Jim likes to look at birds.
   - ○ C. Jim thinks his kite looks like a bird in the sky.

To parents   Go to page 78 and do Activity 1 or 2 with your child.

45

Exercise 40

Read the paragraph. Then fill in the bubble that best completes each sentence.

The Little Toy Boat

May loves to take baths. That is when she can play with her little toy boat. She puts it in the water. Then she splashes in the water to make small waves in the bath. The little boat looks like it sailing in a big ocean. It rocks from side to side, but it never sinks. May loves her little boat.

1. The text is about
   - ○ A. the waves in the bath.
   - ○ B. May's little toy boat.
   - ○ C. a boat sailing in the ocean.

2. A detail that tells more about the main idea is:
   - ○ A. May's boat sails in the ocean.
   - ○ B. May's toy boat rocks from side to side.
   - ○ C. May enjoys bathing.

To parents Go to page 78 and do Activity 1 or 2 with your child.

Making Predictions

Making predictions is one of the many essential reading skills that young readers need to have. A reader who can think ahead to determine what may happen next or how an event may turn out gains a richer understanding of a text. The passages and questions in this section will help your child learn to make reasonable predictions and anticipate probabilities.

This section will provide opportunities for your child to guess what is likely to happen based on information that he already knows as well as the information in the text.

The extension activities provide additional challenges to your child to encourage and develop his understanding of the particular comprehension skill.

Exercise 1

Read the paragraph. Then fill in the bubble that best answers each question.

Hungry Aaron

Aaron is very hungry. He rushes to the kitchen to look for food. He eats a plate of noodles, two pieces of chicken, an apple and a banana. Then he eats a big slice of chocolate cake. He feels very full.

1. Which sentence tells what most likely happens next?
   - ○ A. Aaron will get a stomachache.
   - ○ B. Aaron will eat more food.
   - ○ C. Aaron will play football.

Jada and the Book Sale

Jada loves to read books. She spends her free time reading books. One day, her mother took her to a book sale. There, Jada bought many books. Jada was very excited when she left the book sale. She could not wait to go home.

2. Which sentence tells what most likely happens next?
   - ○ A. Jada will go to bed.
   - ○ B. Jada will start reading her books.
   - ○ C. Jada will go out to the playground.

To parents Go to page 78 and do Activity 3 or 4 with your child.

Exercise 2

Read the paragraph. Then fill in the bubble that best answers each question.

Anton's Eyes

Anton could not see very well. His mother took him to the eye doctor. The doctor told them that Anton needed glasses. Then, his mother bought him a pair of glasses. Anton did not like his glasses. They felt funny on his nose.

1. Which sentence tells what most likely happens next?
   ○ A. Anton will not wear his glasses.
   ○ B. Anton will buy a new pair of glasses.
   ○ C. Anton will visit the doctor again.

Dancing Fun

Anya loved to dance. Every time she heard music, she would start dancing. Her mother took her to a dance studio. There she learned how to dance the Hula. Her teacher told her to practice the new steps at home.

2. Which sentence tells what most likely happens next?
   ○ A. Anya will practice dancing at home.
   ○ B. Anya will listen to music on the radio.
   ○ C. Anya will stop dancing.

To parents Go to page 78 and do Activity 3 or 4 with your child.

Exercise 3

Read the paragraph. Then fill in the bubble that best answers each question.

Jason and the Koala

Jason likes the koala because it is big and furry. When he goes to the zoo, Jason pets and feeds the koala. However, he is not allowed to carry the koala as it may scratch him. One day, Jason secretly tried to carry the koala.

1. Which sentence tells what most likely happens next?
   - ○ A. The koala will scratch Jason.
   - ○ B. Jason will drop the koala.
   - ○ C. Jason will hug the koala.

Thunder and Lightning

Alice heard a loud noise. It sounded like thunder. Alice looked out of the window. She saw lightning. She also felt the wind blowing strongly. Dark clouds covered the sky.

2. Which sentence tells what most likely happens next?
   - ○ A. The sun will shine brightly.
   - ○ B. Alice will go out.
   - ○ C. It will rain heavily.

To parents Go to page 78 and do Activity 3 or 4 with your child.

Exercise 4

Read the paragraph. Then fill in the bubble that best answers each question.

Playing Outside

Aiden and Kyle were playing hide and seek. Kyle was hiding. Aiden was looking everywhere for Kyle. First, he checked behind the closest tree. Next, he looked underneath the bench. Suddenly he saw a shoe near the drain.

1. Which sentence tells what most likely happens next?
   - ○ A. Aiden will fall into the drain.
   - ○ B. Aiden finds Kyle in the drain.
   - ○ C. Aiden picks up the shoe from the drain.

Daddy Talking While Driving

Daddy is driving Jane to school. He is talking on his mobile phone. The other drivers keep honking at Daddy. Jane is very worried. Suddenly, Daddy jams his brakes. Jane is afraid.

2. Which sentence tells what most likely happens next?
   - ○ A. Jane starts crying.
   - ○ B. Daddy starts crying.
   - ○ C. Daddy continues talking

To parents Go to page 78 and do Activity 3 or 4 with your child.

Exercise 5

Read the paragraph. Then fill in the bubble that best answers each question.

Mummy's Cooking

My mother is cooking in the kitchen now. She is frying chicken and some vegetables. She has also cooked some rice. For dessert, Mummy has baked a chocolate cake. This makes my stomach rumble.

1. Which sentence tells what most likely happens next?
   - ○ A. The writer will go out and play.
   - ○ B. The writer will have a good meal.
   - ○ C. The writer will have dessert.

John Loves Eating

John is a big boy. He loves eating. Every day, he eats a large burger meal. He enjoys drinking milkshakes and eating big bars of milk chocolate. Often, he has cookies before going to bed.

2. Which sentence tells what most likely happens next?
   - ○ A. John will become lighter.
   - ○ B. John will become heavier.
   - ○ C. John will win a prize.

To parents Go to page 78 and do Activity 3 or 4 with your child.

Exercise 6

Read the paragraph. Then fill in the bubble that best answers each question.

Alex and His Marbles

Alex loves playing marbles. Every month he buys a new marble. Last month his father bought him some big white marbles. Yesterday, Alex saw a nice set of blue shiny marbles at the mall. He smiled with glee.

1. Which sentence tells what most likely happens next?
   - ○ A. Alex will stop playing marbles.
   - ○ B. Alex will buy the blue marbles.
   - ○ C. Alex will lose his marbles.

Baking a Cake

Joy always wanted to bake her own biscuits and cakes. This was Joy's first try at making a chocolate cake. She beat the eggs and sugar together. But she added too much flour.

2. Which sentence tells what most likely happens next?
   - ○ A. Her cake would taste too sweet.
   - ○ B. Her cake would be too hard.
   - ○ C. Her cake would taste too salty.

To parents Go to page 78 and do Activity 3 or 4 with your child.

53

Exercise 7

Read the paragraph. Then fill in the bubble that best answers each question.

Playing Catch!

Richard and James were playing catch. Richard was determined to catch James. He chased James up and down their street. They did not notice all the tiny stones on the street. James tripped over a large stone.

1. Which sentence tells what most likely happens next?
   - ○ A. James will catch Richard.
   - ○ B. James will keep running.
   - ○ C. James will fall and scrape his knees.

Ghost Stories

Adam's cousins are staying at his house tonight. They start telling each other ghost stories. Adam is very afraid of ghost stories. He does not want to listen to them. But his cousins do not stop talking about ghosts. Adam is very unhappy.

2. Which sentence tells what most likely happens next?
   - ○ A. Adam will sleep well tonight.
   - ○ B. Adam will have a nightmare.
   - ○ C. Adam will tell ghost stories too.

To parents Go to page 78 and do Activity 3 or 4 with your child.

Exercise 8

Read the paragraph. Then fill in the bubble that best answers each question.

The Chicken Coop

Jill's grandmother has a chicken coop. It has five hens in it. However, the front of her chicken coop has a hole. Her grandmother tells her to mend the chicken coop. Jill fixes the hole. She does not see the hole at the back of the chicken coop.

1. Which sentence tells what most likely happens next?
   - ○ A. The hens will run out of the coop.
   - ○ B. Jill's grandmother will be happy with her.
   - ○ C. Jill will be angry with her grandmother.

Brothers

Lucas and Leo are brothers. They are very close to each other. They do everything together. They go to the same school. They have the same friends. One day, Lucas falls and hurts himself.

2. Which sentence tells what most likely happens next?
   - ○ A. Leo will help Lucas up.
   - ○ B. Leo will laugh at Lucas.
   - ○ C. Leo will run away.

To parents Go to page 78 and do Activity 3 or 4 with your child.

Exercise 9

Read the paragraph. Then fill in the bubble that best answers each question.

A Favorite Restaurant

Sally loves to eat fried fish. One day she visits a new restaurant, Karen's Cafe. There she orders fried fish. It is crispy and tasty. Sally is very happy. She has found a place that makes good fish.

1. Which sentence tells what most likely happens next?
   - ○ A. Sally will go to Karen's Cafe often.
   - ○ B. Sally will never return to Karen's Café.
   - ○ C. Sally will find a new place to eat.

Wedding Flowers

Joanna is getting married next week. She loves flowers. Her favorite flowers are sunflowers. Joanna visits the wedding florist. They tell her to have roses, sunflowers or lilies at her wedding. She can only choose one type of flowers.

2. Which sentence tells what most likely happens next?
   - ○ A. Joanna will choose lilies.
   - ○ B. Joanna will choose roses.
   - ○ C. Joanna will choose sunflowers.

To parents   Go to page 78 and do Activity 3 or 4 with your child.

Exercise 10

Read the paragraph. Then fill in the bubble that best answers each question.

Linda's School Concert

Linda school concert is tomorrow. She is very excited. Suddenly, she sneezes. Then she starts coughing. Her mother takes her to the doctor. The doctor gives her some medicine. He tells her to have lots of rest.

1. Which sentence tells what most likely happens next?
   - ○ A. Linda will watch her school concert.
   - ○ B. Linda will stay home and rest.
   - ○ C. Linda will sing at her school concert.

A Cold Drink on a Hot Day

It was a very hot day. Dad was feeling very thirsty. He told me he wanted a cold drink from the kitchen. I went to get Dad iced lemon tea. But there was no lemon to add to the iced tea.

2. Which sentence tells what most likely happens next?
   - ○ A. The writer gets cold water.
   - ○ B. The writer gets iced tea.
   - ○ C. The writer gets hot water.

To parents   Go to page 78 and do Activity 3 or 4 with your child.

Date: _____

Exercise 11

Read the paragraph. Then fill in the bubble that best answers each question.

A Funny Smell

David's mother went to the market last week. She bought some fish to cook for dinner. But she was very busy with work last week. She forgot to cook the food she bought from the market. They were left in the refrigerator.

1. Which sentence tells what most likely happens next?
   ○ A. The food will turn bad.
   ○ B. The refrigerator will stop working.
   ○ C. The food will remain fresh.

My Pet

Ginny loves dogs but she does not have one. She has been begging her father for a dog. Ginny's birthday is coming soon. Her father wants to give her a nice surprise.

2. Which sentence tells what most likely happens next?
   ○ A. Ginny will buy a dog.
   ○ B. Ginny will get a dog for her birthday.
   ○ C. Ginny will get a cat for her birthday.

To parents Go to page 78 and do Activity 3 or 4 with your child.

Date: _____

Exercise 12

Read the paragraph. Then fill in the bubble that best answers each question.

Adrian's Fall

Adrian is an active boy. He cannot keep still. One day, he decides to climb a tree. A branch breaks and he falls to the ground. He lands on his right ankle. Adrian yells in pain!!!

1. Which sentence tells what most likely happens next?
   - ○ A. Adrian will cry.
   - ○ B. Adrian will laugh.
   - ○ C. Adrian will get up and run home.

In the Sick Bed

Dean has not been well for three days. He has a very high fever. He cannot get up from bed. He cannot eat any solid food. He does not feel like talking to anyone. His parents are very worried.

2. Which sentence tells what most likely happens next?
   - ○ A. Dean's parents will let him sleep.
   - ○ B. Dean's parents will take him to the hospital.
   - ○ C. Dean's parents will call the police.

To parents   Go to page 78 and do Activity 3 or 4 with your child.

59

Exercise 13

Read the paragraph. Then fill in the bubble that best answers each question.

Careful, Hot Water!!

Eli was holding a glass of hot water. His baby brother Arien was crawling on the floor. Eli was busy talking to his mother. He did not see Arien in front of him. Oh no!!

1. Which sentence tells what most likely happens next?
   - ○ A. Eli spills the water on Arien.
   - ○ B. Eli drinks the water.
   - ○ C. Arien starts laughing.

A Cuppa, Anyone?

Leon loves to drink tea. He has tea three times a day. He has one cup of tea in the morning, one in the afternoon and one at night. Leon visits a tea shop called T2. He is very happy to find this shop.

2. Which sentence tells what most likely happens next?
   - ○ A. Leon will buy tea at T2.
   - ○ B. Leon will buy coffee at T2.
   - ○ C. Leon will buy cocoa at T2.

To parents Go to page 78 and do Activity 3 or 4 with your child.

Exercise 14

Read the paragraph. Then fill in the bubble that best answers each question.

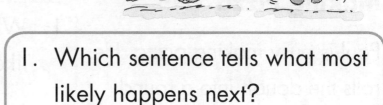

Animal Tails

Pip is a baby elephant. His mother is bigger than him and she walks a lot faster. Pip is worried that he would get lost. He looked around. Pip saw other baby elephants holding onto their mother's tail.

1. Which sentence tells what most likely happens next?
   - ○ A. Pip will get lost.
   - ○ B. Pip will play with the other baby elephants.
   - ○ C. Pip will hold onto his mother's tail.

A Heavy Box

Jarred is carrying a heavy box. It is full of books. He cannot see what is in front of him. He bumps into a table. He accidentally drops the box on his foot.

2. Which sentence tells what most likely happens next?
   - ○ A. Jarred will start to laugh.
   - ○ B. Jarred will start to cry.
   - ○ C. Jarred will start to sing.

To parents   Go to page 78 and do Activity 3 or 4 with your child.

Exercise 15

Read the paragraph. Then fill in the bubble that best answers each question.

Making Pizza

Paul is busy making pizza. He rolls the dough into a round and flat pastry. He sprinkles the ingredients on top of the pastry. He turns the knob on the oven. He can't wait to serve his pizza for dinner.

1. Which sentence tells what most likely happens next?
   - ○ A. Paul puts the pizza into the oven.
   - ○ B. Paul fries the pizza in the frying pan.
   - ○ C. Paul boils the pizza in a saucepan.

What's for Breakfast?

Aaron has breakfast every morning. His mother prepares different food items for him every day. Yesterday, his mother bought a loaf of bread for breakfast.

2. Which sentence tells what most likely happens next?
   - ○ A. Aaron will have pancakes for breakfast.
   - ○ B. Aaron will have cereal for breakfast.
   - ○ C. Aaron will have a sandwich for breakfast.

To parents Go to page 78 and do Activity 3 or 4 with your child.

Exercise 16

Read the paragraph. Then fill in the bubble that best answers each question.

Rolling in the Mud

Jacob and Trey were playing in the rain. They were having fun. While running, they fell in the mud many times. They started throwing mud at each other. They were laughing as they returned home.

1. Which sentence tells what most likely happens next?
   - ○ A. They will do their homework.
   - ○ B. They will have their baths.
   - ○ C. They will go to school.

Up the Stairs Again

Lydia walks up five flights of stairs to take her books. When she reaches the bottom of the stairs, she realizes she has forgotten her pencils. Linda has to walk up five flights of stairs again. Poor Lydia!!!

2. Which sentence tells what most likely happens next?
   - ○ A. Lydia will be tired.
   - ○ B. Lydia will be happy.
   - ○ C. Lydia will be poor.

To parents Go to page 78 and do Activity 3 or 4 with your child.

Exercise 17

Read the paragraph. Then fill in the bubble that best answers each question.

I Forgot My Keys

Shaun woke up late. He drank his coffee quickly. Then he quickly put on his shoes. He was rushing for work. On the way, he realized he did not bring his office keys. He needed them to get into the office.

Hot and Sweaty

Nadine has long hair. Her hair is below her shoulders. During sports, she perspires terribly. In the afternoons, her hair becomes wet. Her mother finally decides to take her to the hairdresser.

1. Which sentence tells what most likely happens next?
   - ○ A. Shaun will go to the office.
   - ○ B. Shaun will go back for his keys.
   - ○ C. Shaun will fall asleep.

2. Which sentence tells what most likely happens next?
   - ○ A. Nadine will have her hair cut.
   - ○ B. Nadine will have her hair permed.
   - ○ C. Nadine's mother will cut her hair.

To parents Go to page 78 and do Activity 3 or 4 with your child.

Exercise 18

Read the paragraph. Then fill in the bubble that best answers each question.

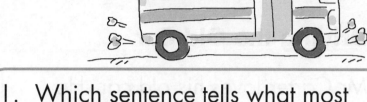

Going to School

My village is 2 kilometers away from my school. There is no public transport where I live. But there is a school bus that takes the village children to school. One day, on the way to school, the school bus breaks down.

1. Which sentence tells what most likely happens next?
   - ○ A. The writer will take the bus to school.
   - ○ B. The writer will walk to school.
   - ○ C. The writer will take a taxi to school.

Ian's Chocolate Feast

Ian's father just returned from Europe. He bought chocolates for Ian. There were all kinds of chocolates with different fillings. Ian couldn't wait to see his friends in school tomorrow.

2. Which sentence tells what most likely happens next?
   - ○ A. Ian will share his chocolates with his friends.
   - ○ B. Ian will eat the chocolates by himself.
   - ○ C. Ian will sell the chocolates.

To parents Go to page 78 and do Activity 3 or 4 with your child.

Exercise 19

Read the paragraph. Then fill in the bubble that best answers each question.

Driving the Old Car

Mr Carter loves his old car. He does not want to sell it. One day, as he was driving, he heard "clink, clink, clink", and the car started to wobble. Then he saw smoke coming out of his car and it stopped. He turned the key again and again but the car would not start.

1. Which sentence tells what most likely happens next?
   - ○ A. Mr Carter will sell his car.
   - ○ B. Mr Carter's car will start.
   - ○ C. Mr Carter will change the tire.

Something Nice

Linda's class wanted to start something new in school. They chose a day when each person would do something nice for someone else in their class. Linda knew that John was upset because he lost his pet hamster.

2. Which sentence tells what most likely happens next?
   - ○ A. Linda will laugh at John.
   - ○ B. Linda will do something nice for herself.
   - ○ C. Linda will do something nice for John.

To parents Go to page 78 and do Activity 3 or 4 with your child.

Exercise 20

Read the paragraph. Then fill in the bubble that best answers each question.

Leah's Voice

Leah has lost her voice. She finds it painful to speak. Her throat feels dry. Her mother tells her to drink more water. Leah does not like to drink water. Water is tasteless. Her mother has an idea.

1. Which sentence tells what most likely happens next?
   - ○ A. Leah's mother gives her orange juice to drink.
   - ○ B. Leah's mother gives her bread.
   - ○ C. Leah's mother says Leah does not need to drink.

Rain Rain Go Away!!

Dina is looking forward to go out and play. She has a new pair of roller blades. Her roller blades are red. They look awesome. When Dina steps out of her house, she sees dark clouds and feels raindrops.

2. Which sentence tells what most likely happens next?
   - ○ A. Dina will go out and play on her roller blades.
   - ○ B. Dina will go back indoors.
   - ○ C. Dina will bring an umbrella.

To parents   Go to page 78 and do Activity 3 or 4 with your child.

Exercise 21

Read the paragraph. Then fill in the bubble that best answers each question.

A New Sport

Grant wants to learn a new sport. He loves going out in the snow and having fun. He already knows how to ski. Then he sees a sports program and he sees someone snowboarding. It looks like it's a lot of fun.

1. Which sentence tells what most likely happens next?
   ○ A. Grant will going skiing.
   ○ B. Grant will make a snowman.
   ○ C. Grant will learn snowboarding.

Making New Friends

It was Jamie's first day at her new school. She felt lost. She missed her friends at her old school. The teacher introduced her in class and she took her seat. During the break a girl named Rachel asked Jamie to join her for break time.

2. Which sentence tells what most likely happens next?
   ○ A. Jamie and Rachel will become friends.
   ○ B. Jamie and Rachel will quarrel.
   ○ C. Jamie will say no.

To parents   Go to page 78 and do Activity 3 or 4 with your child.

Date: _____

Exercise 22

Read the paragraph. Then fill in the bubble that best answers each question.

Daddy is Sound Asleep

Daddy has an important meeting at work. He is still sleeping. He is snoring very loudly. Daddy must be very tired. He went to bed very late last night. He was preparing for the meeting.

1. Which sentence tells what most likely happens next?
   ○ A. Daddy will be late for his meeting.
   ○ B. Daddy will not go to work that day.
   ○ C. Daddy will be happy when he wakes up.

An Exciting Holiday

Jim had an exciting holiday at Swallow Falls. At the waterfall, there was a 'No Swimming' sign. A group of disobedient children were splashing around in the water. Suddenly, one of the girls screamed.

2. Which sentence tells what most likely happens next?
   ○ A. Jim will help the girl.
   ○ B. Jim will laugh at the girl.
   ○ C. Jim will run away.

To parents Go to page 78 and do Activity 3 or 4 with your child.

Exercise 23

Read the paragraph. Then fill in the bubble that best answers each question.

A Beautiful Birthday Card

Aunt May sent Janice a beautiful card for her birthday. It had a picture of a birthday cake. There was also money inside the card. Janice was overjoyed!! She ran to the telephone to call Aunt May.

1. Which sentence tells what most likely happens next?
   - ○ A. Janice will thank Aunt May.
   - ○ B. Janice will go shopping.
   - ○ C. Janice will buy herself a gift.

A Little Bird is Hurt

Noah and Lily were playing in the field. They saw an injured bird on the ground. It was a sparrow. Noah gently picked up the bird. They take it home to their mother.

2. Which sentence tells what most likely happens next?
   - ○ A. Their mother cleans the bird's wound.
   - ○ B. They play with the bird.
   - ○ C. They place the bird in a box.

To parents Go to page 78 and do Activity 3 or 4 with your child.

Exercise 24

Read the paragraph. Then fill in the bubble that best answers each question.

Speedy

Speedy is a racehorse. She won many races and many medals. She runs very fast and she is a gentle horse. Her owner, Mr Michaels, loves Speedy, but Speedy is getting old. She runs slower now and seldom wins any of her races.

1. Which sentence tells what most likely happens next?
   - ○ A. Speedy will race more often.
   - ○ B. Speedy will win more medals.
   - ○ C. Speedy will retire.

Liam and His Bicycle

Liam was cycling to school. He was enjoying himself. Suddenly, a car knocked him down. Liam screamed in pain. The driver of the car helped him sit up. The driver used his phone to call an ambulance.

2. Which sentence tells what most likely happens next?
   - ○ A. Liam is taken to the hospital.
   - ○ B. Liam is taken to a police station.
   - ○ C. Liam is taken home.

To parents Go to page 78 and do Activity 3 or 4 with your child.

Exercise 25

Read the paragraph. Then fill in the bubble
that best answers each question.

Class Duty Roster

Everyone in my class has a
daily duty. My duty is to sweep
the floor. Sophia is not in school
today. She is sick. Her duty is
to clean the board. Our teacher
asks me to help Sophia.

1. Which sentence tells what
   most likely happens next?
   ○ A. The writer will call
      Sophia.
   ○ B. The teacher will clean
      the board.
   ○ C. The writer will clean
      the board.

Things in the Trunk

We are going to visit
Grandma. We have a lot of
things for her. We have six
bags. Mummy places all the
bags into the trunk of the car.
The trunk is full. One of
the bags is sticking out of
the trunk.

2. Which sentence tells what most
   likely happens next?
   ○ A. Mummy will put one bag
      on the back seat.
   ○ B. They will only bring
      five bags.
   ○ C. They will stay home.

To parents   Go to page 78 and do Activity 3 or 4 with your child.

Exercise 26

Read the paragraph. Then fill in the bubble that best answers each question.

Ironing Clothes

Gina irons her clothes every Sunday. She listens to music while ironing. Sometimes, she dances to the music. This time she left the hot iron on her green blouse.

1. Which sentence tells what most likely happens next?
   ○ A. Gina's green pants will be burnt.
   ○ B. Gina's blue blouse will be burnt.
   ○ C. Gina's green blouse will be burnt.

A Trip to the Wildlife Park

Joe went to the Featherdale Wildlife Park with his parents. He enjoyed himself. He saw many different animals. The best part of the trip was feeding the kangaroos. It was very thrilling. But he did not have time to see the koalas.

2. Which sentence tells what most likely happens next?
   ○ A. Joe returns to the park another day to see the koalas.
   ○ B. Joe spends the night at the park.
   ○ C. Joe takes a koala home with him.

To parents Go to page 78 and do Activity 3 or 4 with your child.

Date: _____

Exercise 27

Read the paragraph. Then fill in the bubble that best answers each question.

The Lost Shoe

Carl was fast asleep in the car. It was a long drive along the countryside. His little brother Chris, took Carl's shoe and threw it out of the window. Carl felt someone tugging at his foot. He woke up and saw that his favorite shoe was missing.

1. Which sentence tells what most likely happens next?
   ○ A. Chris will give Carl his shoes.
   ○ B. Carl will throw Chris's shoes out of the car.
   ○ C. Carl will ask their parents to stop the car.

Too Much Homework

Celia was very tired. She longed to go to sleep. She could not rest because she had too much homework. She had homework for all her subjects. It was going to be a long night!!!

2. Which sentence tells what most likely happens next?
   ○ A. Celia will sleep late.
   ○ B. Celia will sleep early.
   ○ C. Celia will watch television.

To parents Go to page 78 and do Activity 3 or 4 with your child.

74

Exercise 28

Read the paragraph. Then fill in the bubble that best answers each question.

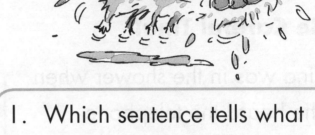

Stop Buster!

David wants to give his dog, Buster, a bath. Buster hates bath time. He doesn't like being wet. David catches Buster and puts him in the bath. The moment Buster comes out of the tub, he shakes off all the water.

1. Which sentence tells what most likely happens next?
   ○ A. David will get wet.
   ○ B. Buster will need another bath.
   ○ C. Buster will jump back into the tub.

A Friend to Jog With

Jen wanted to take part in a marathon. She would have to train hard. Jen decided to start jogging. She wished she didn't have to jog alone. She heard that Tom was going to run in the marathon too.

2. Which sentence tells what most likely happens next?
   ○ A. Jen will jog alone.
   ○ B. Jen will ask Tom to jog with her.
   ○ C. Jen will not exercise.

To parents Go to page 78 and do Activity 3 or 4 with your child.

Exercise 29

Read the paragraph. Then fill in the bubble that best answers each question.

Be Careful Tina!

Tina was in the shower when she heard the telephone ringing. She had soap all over her body. She did not want to miss the call. She ran to pick up the phone.

1. Which sentence tells what most likely happens next?
   - ○ A. Tina misses the call.
   - ○ B. Tina slips and falls.
   - ○ C. Tina answers the call.

Going Home to Mum and Dad

Jeff is excited. He is going to pay his parents a surprise visit. He buys a ticket for the 8am bus. He thinks he will be there by 10am. But his bus is delayed by 3 hours.

2. Which sentence tells what most likely happens next?
   - ○ A. Jeff will have to buy another ticket.
   - ○ B. Jeff will miss the bus.
   - ○ C. Jeff will get there in the afternoon.

To parents   Go to page 78 and do Activity 3 or 4 with your child.

Exercise 30

Read the paragraph. Then fill in the bubble that best answers each question.

Working in a Factory

Dad works in a factory near our home. He makes car parts. Every day, he breathes in the smoke from the factory. This is not good for him. I wish he would get another job.

1. Which sentence tells what most likely happens next?
   - ○ A. Dad will have a bad cough.
   - ○ B. Dad will have a cold.
   - ○ C. Dad will lose his job.

Good Manners

Lynn was in the bus with her friends. They were sitting down and laughing with each other. At one stop, Lynn saw an old lady come on the bus. It was a full bus. There were no vacant seats.

2. Which sentence tells what most likely happens next?
   - ○ A. The old lady will get off the bus.
   - ○ B. Lynn will laugh at the old lady.
   - ○ C. Lynn will offer the old lady her seat.

To parents   Go to page 78 and do Activity 3 or 4 with your child.

Extension Activities

Activity 1: Finding the Details

Skill: Identifying main idea and details

Re-read each paragraph with your child. Your child is required to identify only one detail. Ask him to find other details that support the main idea in the paragraph. Underline each detail in a different color.

Activity 2: What's the Big Idea?

Skill: Identifying main idea and details
Choose some simple non-fiction paragraphs. Read the paragraph with your child. Then, ask him to identify the main idea of each paragraph.

Activity 3: Picture Forward

Skill: Making Predictions
Choose a picture book. As you flip through the pages, ask your child to use the pictures to predict what would happen next in the story. Then read the text to check if his prediction is accurate.

Activity 4: What's in a Title?

Skill: Making Predictions
Choose some storybooks. Challenge your child to think about what the story could be about based on the title and the illustrations.

Answer Key

Page 7

1. B 2. B

Page 8

1. C 2. C

Page 9

1. B 2. C

Page 10

1. C 2. C

Page 11

1. C 2. B

Page 12

1. C 2. C

Page 13

1. C 2. B

Page 14

1. A 2. B

Page 15

1. B 2. C

Page 16

1. B 2. C

Page 17

1. B 2. C

Page 18

1. A 2. A

Page 19

1. B 2. A

Page 20

1. C 2. B

Page 21

1. B 2. B

Page 22

1. B 2. C

Page 23

1. B 2. B

Page 24

1. C 2. A

Page 25

1. C 2. B

Page 26

1. B 2. A

Page 27

1. B 2. A

Page 28

1. B 2. C

Page 29

1. C 2. A

Page 30

1. C 2. B

Page 31

1. B 2. C

Page 32

1. C 2. B

Page 33

1. C 2. A

Page 34

1. A 2. A

Page 35

1. A 2. A

Page 36

1. B 2. A

Page 37

1. B 2. B

Page 38

1. A 2. A

Page 39

1. B   2. C

Page 40

1. B   2. B

Page 41

1. C   2. B

Page 42

1. C   2. A

Page 43

1. A   2. A

Page 44

1. B   2. B

Page 45

1. C   2. C

Page 46

1. B   2. B

Page 48

1. A   2. B

Page 49

1. A   2. A

Page 50

1. A   2. C

Page 51

1. B   2. A

Page 52

1. B   2. B

Page 53

1. B   2. B

Page 54

1. C   2. B

Page 55

1. A   2. A

Page 56

1. A   2. C

Page 57

1. B   2. B

Page 58

1. A   2. B

Page 59

1. A   2. B

Page 60

1. A   2. A

Page 61

1. B   2. B

Page 62

1. A   2. C

Page 63

1. B   2. A

Page 64

1. B   2. C

Page 65

1. B   2. A

Page 66

1. C   2. C

Page 67

1. A   2. B

Page 68

1. C   2. A

Page 69

1. A   2. A

Page 70

1. A   2. A

Page 71

1. A   2. C

Page 72

1. C   2. B

Page 73

1. C   2. A

Page 74

1. B   2. A

Page 75

1. A   2. B

Page 76

1. B   2. C

Page 77

1. A   2. C